A WILDLIFE GUIDE
DENALI NATIONAL PARK & PRESERVE, ALASKA

CRAIG BRANDT

BY KRIS CAPPS

HENRY HOLDSWORTH

services

Produced for
ARA Leisure Services, Inc.
by Companion Press

Santa Barbara, California
Jane Freeburg, Publisher/Editor
Designed by Lucy Brown
Printed and bound in Korea through
Bolton Associates, San Rafael, California

ISBN 0-944917-32-9

9 8 7 6 5 4 3 2 1

ROY M. CORRAL

ROBIN BRANDT

CONTENTS

PART ONE
A Pristine Place

KATHY BUSHUE

A light dusting of snow decorates the autumn tundra foreground of the Alaska Range, opposite. Dwarfed by the landscape, a hiker, above, views Polychrome Pass.

For fifteen years, Wildlife Tour Driver Jeralyn Hath has guided visitors through Denali National Park and Preserve. She never tires of these daily trips into the heart of the Alaska Range, for each journey is different. On every tour, somewhere along the park road, she stumbles upon special moments—a newborn moose calf wobbling behind its mother; a wolf oblivious to cameras clicking as it relentlessly digs for a ground squirrel at the side of the road; or a swath of dwarf fireweed setting river banks afire with brilliant color.

For the wildlife that inhabits Denali, life is much the same today as it was thousands of years ago. The animals go about their daily lives without interruption, as they have always done. This is a pristine place. "It's true wilderness," notes Hath. "People come into the park and they realize how really rare true wilderness is in the world." In 1974 the United Nations designated Denali National Park and Preserve an International Biosphere Reserve, a unique area where the natural world can be studied and observed on its own terms, without human intervention.

Denali's vastness can seem overwhelming to a newcomer. Miles of tundra stretch out to meet rugged peaks on the horizon. Glacial streams dance down those distant mountains, then fan out in cold tendrils, carving new and numerous channels. Splotches of color dot the landscape where tenacious wildflowers hug the ground like a colorful carpet. Their growing season is short, but critical, since flowering plants provide nutrients to the many animals that feed upon them. That plaintive whistle you hear could be a golden plover that has flown from South America to nest here. Yet another distinctive call harkens from an arctic warbler, a tiny traveler all the way from Asia. Denali National Park is home to 161 species of birds, 37 species of mammals, and 450 species of plants.

Mount McKinley, at 20,320 feet the highest mountain in North America, looms over it all. Alaskans often refer to it simply as "The Mountain." During summer months, this imposing peak creates its own weather system and may be visible only about one-third of the time. But when the mountain is "out," there is no doubt which peak to identify as McKinley. It overshadows the surrounding peaks of the Alaska Range, its massive flanks filling the horizon.

The first glimpse of "The Mountain" comes just about eight miles into the park as you pass from the forest into the tundra. At that point, it looms large even 72 miles away. A prospector dubbed the mountain "McKinley" in 1896, in honor of William McKinley of Ohio, who became the 25th president of the United States. Long ago, Athabascan Indians called it "Denali," which means "the high one." Alaskans today call it by

both names. Debate continues as to whether the mountain should be "officially" renamed Denali.

Climbing Mount McKinley is serious business. More than a thousand climbers attempt to scale its slopes every year; about half of them succeed. So far, 76 climbers have died trying. Most climbers begin their expedition from the Kahiltna Glacier at 7,200 feet, and allow between twenty and thirty days for the attempt. McKinley is not only high, but bitterly cold. Severe storms hit regularly with little warning, and winds sometimes gust to 150 mph. Two of the best climbers in the world, Dougal Haston and Doug Scott, veterans of ascents in the Himalayas, observed after scaling the South Face of McKinley in 1976: "We were drawing heavily on all our Himalayan experience

A double rainbow, above, emerges from stormy skies over Teklanika Flats, not an uncommon sight some summer afternoons. Opposite: A splash of colorful flowers drift across a gravel bar on the Thorofare River; Mount McKinley looms in the background.

just to survive and it was a respectful pair that finally stood on the summit ridge. Everything was cold, even our souls."

Denali National Park wasn't created solely because of the mountain, however, but to preserve and protect the wildlife at its base. Much of the credit goes to Charles Sheldon, an avid naturalist, conservationist, and hunter, who came to the area in 1906 to study Dall sheep. Impressed by the profusion of wildlife, he returned the following year with guide Harry Karstens, who eventually became the park's first superintendent. They built a cabin on the upper Toklat River and spent the winter there, extensively scrutinizing the land and its wildlife.

Sheldon watched hunters kill more and more animals to feed residents of nearby growing communities like Nenana, Kantishna and Fairbanks. A railroad would soon be built and he feared the arrival of additional hunters might devastate wildlife populations. Sheldon returned to the East and used his influential position with the renowned Boone and Crockett Club to campaign for creation of a wildlife refuge at Denali. His efforts finally paid off in 1917, when, with the flourish of a pen, President Woodrow Wilson established Mount McKinley National Park. Sheldon remained disappointed, though, that the new park wasn't called Denali National Park.

The official name change from Mount McKinley National Park to Denali National Park and Preserve finally came in 1980, when the park more than tripled in size from 1.9 million acres to 6 million acres, roughly the size of Massachusetts. The park now encompasses the entire Mount McKinley massif and the Denali caribou herd's wintering and calving grounds.

MICHAEL H. FRANCIS

There were few visitors in the park's early years, when the railroad provided the only transportation. Only few thousand tourists traveled here, a handful by private rail cars. The National Park Service constructed the park road between 1923 and 1938. Today, the 92-mile park road is maintained only during the summer months, usually from mid-June to mid-September. To limit traffic and lessen impact on wildlife populations, a shuttle bus system ferries visitors into the park. Private vehicles are restricted. The park road remains the sole gateway to this wilderness.

20,320-foot Mount McKinley, above, veiled in drifting clouds. "The Mountain" creates its own weather, often hidden from view. Park visitors may see the peak on about one-third of summer days.

Photographed at midnight in mid-summer, the Teklanika River glows with intense blue light.

ROBIN BRANDT

FRANK S. BALTHIS

PART TWO
Magnificent Wildlife

A bull caribou moves through the tundra near Sable Pass, opposite. The park road near the Savage River, above right, leads through September color.

Like a ribbon, the road into Denali National Park and Preserve stretches and winds through a corridor rich in its wildness, up and over mountain passes, and through taiga and tundra. *Taiga,* a Russian word for moist coniferous woodlands at high latitudes, describes Denali's forests of white and black spruce interspersed with aspen and balsam poplar trees. Woodlands seen from the park road include white spruce, which grow in dry soil. Elsewhere in the park, black spruce survive in boggier areas, growing sparse and spindly. Within the shelter of these forests live snowshoe hares and lynx, great-horned owls, red squirrels, gray jays and magpies.

Above timberline, between 2,700 and 3,000 feet in Denali, the tundra rolls out like a lumpy carpet. There are no tall trees here. Instead, a miniature forest grows—dwarf birch, flowering plants, willow, alders, grasses and sedges, mosses and lichens. In the alpine tundra, soil is scarce and flowers cling to rocky slopes; vegetation is a thin veneer.

Boreal forest and Double Mountain reflect in the still waters of a pond near Teklanika, opposite. Above left: only shreds remain of the rich velvet covering, filled with blood vessels, that nourished this caribou bull's antlers as they grew. A grizzly bear, above right, traverses autumn tundra.

As fall approaches, berries ripen. Blueberries, popular with both people and animals, can be found anywhere in the forest or the tundra. Cranberries usually grow in the forest. And the bear's favorite—soap berries, which are high in fat content—grow on gravel bars, woods, or mountain slopes.

Except for those made by wildlife over the aeons, and a few man-made trails around the headquarters area, there are no trails at Denali National Park. In this true wilderness, hikers must choose for themselves the easiest and quickest way to get where they're going. That means taking advantage of natural features, like river beds or rocky ridges, where walking is easier.

Denali National Park sometimes finds itself dubbed the Serengeti of the North, but that can be misleading. Don't expect to see great herds of caribou or roving packs of wolves. Keep in mind that all wildlife sightings in the park are a matter of exquisite timing, sharp eyes, and good fortune.

Denali National Park's environment is really a sub-arctic desert—it can't support huge numbers of animals. Only about fifteen inches of precipitation falls at Denali National Park every year, two-thirds of that during summer months. The landscape may look lush, but that is only because permafrost, or frozen soil, prevents the moisture from sinking into the ground. Moisture saturates that thin layer atop the frozen soil.

ERWIN & PEGGY BAUER

Although the land is vast, food is limited during winter months. The eight to nine months of winter can be harsh. There are no snakes or lizards at Denali; these creatures wouldn't survive winter. (Biologists are still studying how one amphibian, a wood frog, manages to make Denali home.) Researchers estimate the northern part of Denali National Park's six million acres currently sustain 2,600 moose, 1,700 caribou and 200 to 300 grizzly bears. Those numbers are always changing.

Visitors must adjust their vision to the large scale of distance in Denali. From a place like Polychrome Pass, the vista seems never-ending.

The road becomes a trail, sometimes shared with wildlife. Keep a watchful eye. To see wild animals close to the road is a special experience. It's also a matter of timing: a bus in the right place at the right time—and someone looking in the right spot, at the right time.

What better reminder that this is not a zoo. These animals may seem accustomed to seeing the buses drive by, but they are still wild animals and should never be approached. For most of the year the buses aren't there, and Denali National Park's wildlife engages in a daily life and death struggle for survival out of our view.

Above, even a large and powerful grizzly bear seems miniscule in this vast land. A bear grazes on grasses of the open tundra, one of its favorite feeding areas. Opposite: a band of Dall sheep peer down at the park road far below. From the road, the sheep will look like tiny specks of white.

KAREN JETTMAR

With the Alaska Range providing a spectacular backdrop, a cow moose feeds in Wonder Lake, located near the end of the park's 92-mile road.

MOOSE

Moose are the first big mammals visitors are likely to encounter as the bus drives out the park road. These ungainly creatures often gather near woodlands not far from park headquarters; they like to bed down among the trees. Awkward-looking with a large drooping nose, moose are the largest animal at Denali. Bulls reach record weights of 1,500 pounds, and stand as tall as 7½ feet at the shoulder. They browse on willow leaves and stems—up to sixty pounds a day. Although they occasionally wander above timberline, moose are generally found at lower elevations.

Moose often choose the area near the park entrance to give birth to their calves. Twin moose calves are common, and triplets are not unheard of. Born in May and June, moose calves stay with their mothers for a year. Moose cows are fiercely protective of their young. Don't make the mistake of approaching a cow and calf, or of getting between a mother and her offspring. If a moose puts its ears back and raises the hair on the back of its neck, it is ready to charge and strike with swift, potentially deadly hooves. Don't underestimate a moose's power or ability to inflict injury.

A bull moose grunts as he makes his way through heavy snow, above left. Above right, a moose cow and calf graze for aquatic plants. Right, moose primarily feed on willow, and are often found near woodlands.

Karen Jettmar

Michael Giannechini

Martin W. Grosnick

Caribou

The always-moving caribou can be seen almost anywhere in the park, nose to the ground, slowly grazing as they walk. They feed on a variety of plants during the summer; primarily on lichens during winter months.

About forty years ago, Denali's caribou herd was massive—as many as 30,000 animals. For reasons biologists still don't understand, that number has fluctuated and declined over the years to fewer than 2,000 in 1993. Driven by insects that keep them on the move, caribou often seek out windy sites that will keep warble flies and nostril flies at bay. They can often be spotted on patches of snow at higher elevations.

Both male and female caribou grow antlers, the only deer that do so. The bulls' antlers are significantly larger than females. During fall, bulls can also be identified by a prominent white mantle that covers the neck and part of the shoulders.

Caribou often seek snow patches, above, to escape harassing insects or heat. Both bulls and cows grow antlers. Top left, autumn signals the approach of the mating season. Below left, bulls spar over females.

JEFF GNASS

How much do those antlers weigh? As much as 25 pounds or more on big bulls. Caribou drop the antlers and grow a new pair every year. Rodents often gnaw on discarded antlers for nourishment.

Bull moose and caribou grow new antlers every year. Depending how old the animals are and how abundant the food supply, the antlers grow more majestic every season. A soft coating called velvet covers the antlers and holds the blood supply that nurtures them as they grow. When winter approaches, the animals rub their antlers against trees and bushes, ripping off the velvet, revealing bright red antlers underneath. Bulls then challenge each other with lowered heads, seeking the privilege of mating with avail-

able females. In this way, only the strongest genes pass on to the next generation. This mating season, called the rut, takes place in October.

Bull moose and bull caribou drop their antlers in December and January. Female caribou who aren't pregnant keep their antlers longer, and most pregnant caribou hold on to their antlers until calving time in early summer, when the cows give birth to a single calf. Caribou calves walk just an hour after birth and are capable of running on their second day of life.

ROBIN BRANDT

MICHAEL GIANNECHINI

DALL SHEEP

Look up at the ridgetops to spot tiny specks of white, clinging to precipitous footing. The agile, elusive Dall sheep captivated naturalist Charles Sheldon, who came to Denali in 1906 to study them. Like the Dall porpoise, the sheep were named after William Healey Dall, an early naturalist who explored parts of Alaska in the late 1800s. Sheep are quite different animals than goats, who have deeper chests, longer hair that grows over their legs like pantaloons, and black horns.

Dall sheep rarely stray from the high country, except when moving from summer to winter grazing grounds. Then, they quickly and nervously step into the lowlands and make their way across valleys. The sheep spend summers in mountains on both sides of the park road, then move to the park's northern regions, where lighter snowfall provides better grazing during winter months.

Male and female Dall sheep usually don't mingle until the November–December mating season. Ewes give birth in May or June and lambs can be seen romping on rocky slopes throughout

KATHY BUSHUE

the summer. Dall sheep never shed their horns, which are made of the same substance as your fingernails—keratin. A sheep's age can be determined by counting the rings on its horns. The ewes' horns are short, slender, and slightly curved; as rams mature, their thicker, heavier horns form a circle when seen from the side. A "full curl" ram may be seven or eight years old.

A newborn lamb, top left, peeks out from beneath its mother. Newborn Dall sheep weigh five to seven pounds and can stand within the first hour. Top right, annual growth rings on a ram's horns indicate the animal's age. Intense battles by head-butting, left, determine dominance and which rams will mate. Opposite, ewes and lambs spend most of the year apart from the rams, ever watchful for predators.

23

MICHAEL H. FRANCIS

CRAIG BRANDT

ALISSA CRANDALL

Opposite: 200 to 300 grizzly bears roam the wild country of Denali. The bears thrive here where they have the space to live undisturbed. Above, grizzly cubs are generally dark-colored their first year of life. A grizzly family, above center, feasts on grasses and roots, which make up most of a bear's diet. Above right, a bear takes a back-scratching break right on the park road.

BEARS

Denali National Park remains one of the few places in the world where visitors can see grizzly bears in the wild. (Black bears, which also live in Denali, are rarely visible from the park road.) Grizzlies range in color from light brown to black—many are a distinctive bleached-blond color—with a prominent shoulder hump and long, curved claws. On the open tundra, digging for roots, a bear can look like a haystack on the hillside. Yet grizzlies move across the landscape with surprising swiftness. In short bursts, they can reach speeds of 35 to 40 miles per hour.

Grizzly and brown bears are the same species, but brown bears generally live on the coast while grizzlies live inland. Grizzlies are not as large as their brown counterparts, who feast on a rich coastal diet of fish. In Denali, plants make up much of the grizzly bear's diet. Still, a bear may expend a tremendous amount of energy trying to extricate a ground squirrel from its underground tunnel: each consumed ground squirrel is a 2,000-calorie meal.

In the spring, grizzlies will prey on moose and caribou calves. They also scavenge carcasses, and can thwart hungry wolves by running them off a recently killed animal. But bears aren't always the victors in these standoffs. One biologist theorized that the hungriest contender usually wins. Bears sleep through the winter with a slightly reduced temperature and no need for food. They can awaken at any time and often come out of the den during warm spells.

GRIZZLY BEAR

GRIZZLY BEARS ARE DANGEROUS

Bears can be seen anywhere in the park. A few seasons ago, a grizzly bear tussled with a moose, right through the residential area near park headquarters. The bear eventually killed the moose in nearby woods, putting a crimp on children trick-or-treating from house to house that Halloween night. The open tundra of Sable Pass is prime grizzly bear habitat. In an effort to maintain this area in its pristine state, and to ensure the bears have a place where they can never be disturbed, the Sable Pass area is closed to hiking.

Biologists believe that grizzly bears need a tremendous amount of space to range in search of sustenance. How much space depends on habitat and availability of food. At Denali, biologists estimate that female bears typically need a range of 40 to 150 square miles and males need a range of 270 to 350 square miles.

Summer breezes don't bother this blond grizzly, above. Bears investigate a sign on Sable Pass, top left, an area where hiking is prohibited. Left, caught in an intimate moment, a sow nurses her cubs.

MARTIN H. GROSNICK

MICHAEL H. FRANCIS

CRAIG BRANDT

TOM & PAT LEESON

WOLVES AND FOXES

Wolves have been sighted regularly at Denali National Park in recent years, hunting near the road or feeding on carcasses. Some wolves wear radio collars as part of a scientific study. (Although one visitor insisted the canine digging next to the road had to be a dog, since it wore a collar; remember that Denali National Park's wolves are indeed wild.)

Wolves can range in color from black to white, but most are gray. They hunt for caribou, moose, and even Dall sheep, but much of their diet consists of ptarmigan, squirrels, and other rodents. Before choosing a specific caribou for prey, wolves hunting in a pack will often shadow a group of caribou, chasing them, to determine whether an attack will succeed.

It's not unusual to see a red fox hunting along the park road, perhaps with a ptarmigan or arctic ground squirrel already clenched in its jaws. Like the wolf, this swift hunter remains active all winter.

A wolf feeds on a sheep carcass, top. Center, wolves howl to communicate with each other. Top right, wolves often hunt alone, but also join forces with other members of the pack to bring down prey. Below right, foxes feed largely on mice, ptarmigan, and squirrels.

SMALL MAMMALS

The most commonly seen mammal in the park is also probably the most important in Denali's food chain—the arctic ground squirrel. A consistently high population of these squirrels provides a dependable source of food for larger animals, including golden eagles, red fox, wolves, lynx, wolverines, and bears. These little sentinels, who sound alarm with a loud chirp, dig an intricate tunnel system with numerous entrances and exits to escape predators. Ground squirrels spend winter in their burrows in deep hibernation. A squirrel's temperature drops below freezing during the winter months, a unique adaptation to the subarctic environment.

Along rocky talus slopes live tiny pikas. These four-inch members of the rabbit clan weigh only a few ounces. Throughout the summer, pikas collect flowers and grasses and cache them for winter storage. When disturbed, the pika emits a high-pitched squeak or whistle before disappearing into its rocky sanctuary. Pikas remain active throughout the winter.

Hoary marmots, chubby rodents related to squirrels—but much larger in size—can grow up to 20 pounds. Males and females mate for life, building dens among piles of heavy rocks and boulders. In winter, marmots snuggle underground in groups of as many as fifteen animals. Their body temperature drops to just above freezing; other body processes become barely perceptible.

RICK MCINTYRE

DIANA STRATTON

MICHAEL GIANNECHINI

RICHARD HAMILTON SMITH

Marmots, above left, mate for life and live in family units. They keep their young for at least two years, and greet each other with what looks like a kiss. Left, arctic ground squirrels are always on the alert for danger. They have to be— they are the prime food for many park predators. The pika, top, "makes hay" all summer, carefully drying stashes of grasses in rocky niches so it will have food for winter. The showshoe hare, above, changes color both winter and summer to blend in with its surroundings.

The long-tailed jaeger, top right, spends summers in Denali and winters in the central Pacific or near Japan, flying inland only to nest. Right, a rock ptarmigan and its chick blend with the vegetation. Below right, the willow ptarmigan, Alaska's state bird, changes plumage for the winter. Below, a hawk owl lives in the taiga forest and hunts shrews, birds, and squirrels.

BIRDS

Birds come from all over the world to nest at Denali, where rare species can often be easily spotted. Northern Wheatears, for instance, fly to Denali from Africa. Arctic terns complete a 20,000-mile roundtrip commute from Antarctica every year, and long-tailed jaegers enjoy summer at Denali and life at sea in the southern oceans every winter. Mew gulls, who look more at home on the beach than on the tundra, fly inland to nest at Denali. Gyrfalcons, arctic warblers, and others arrive every year. At Denali, prime nesting sites are readily available for many species, whether they choose the open tundra or the camouflage of a gravel bar.

All three kinds of ptarmigan—willow, rock, and white-tailed—live at Denali year round, changing colors with the seasons, blending with their surroundings. Thick feathers cover their feet, a warm adaptation for Alaska's cold winters. Frequently spotted at road's edge, ptarmigan can also be found in forests or on the open tundra. Along with ptarmigan, birds that spend all winter here include magpies, gray jays, and ravens.

WILDFLOWERS

The flowers of Denali provide a cavalcade of color, especially in mid-summer. Plants of the same species may flourish as much as six weeks apart, depending on their location. For example, flowers on south-facing slopes will receive more sunlight, so they will bloom before plants on cooler, north-facing slopes. Bright pink fireweed, one profuse and obvious flower in Denali National Park, blooms from the bottom of the stem. Alaskans say when the fireweed's top flowers open, summer is over. It isn't unusual for dwarf fireweed, also known as river beauty, to blanket gravel bars along glacial streams, painting a bright pink wash through the landscape.

While fireweed signals the end of the season, the purple pasque flower, or spring crocus, usually signals the onset of spring. In between, a plethora of wildflowers can be found throughout the park, sometimes in suprising places: the crevice of a rock, the top of a ridge, the middle of the tundra. Ground squirrels, marmots and other rodents depend heavily on flowers for food.

It may be hard to pick out individual wild-flowers from the bus window, but one recently introduced roadside flower may look familiar to most people—the dandelion. A common sight on lawns across America, dandelions are fairly new to Denali. These yellow flowers appeared shortly after the Parks Highway opened in 1972. They commonly grow along the park road now and are progressing westward, into the park.

Alpine forget-me-not

Moss campion

Mountain avens

Kinnickinnik and crowberry

Spring beauty

Mushrooms and lichens

Background: Tundra foliage, Brett Baunton
Opposite: Fireweed, Richard Hamilton Smith

ROBIN BRANDT

CRAIG BRANDT

What is the best time of year to visit Denali? It depends what you want to see. In June, snow still clings to mountainsides and grasses have yet to turn green. But Denali's wild residents are giving birth and the wonder of new life is evident. July is wildflower season. In August, rain falls more readily, and the tundra glows red, gold and orange as colors change. Animals appear at their prime as they prepare for cold months ahead, with thick, shiny coats, and full-grown antlers. Grizzly bears are fattened up for their winter sleep and weasels, snowshoe hares and ptarmigan are about to change colors and don white coats.

And then, there's winter. When the last visitor departs, and snow begins to fall, Denali rests under a soft, quiet blanket of white. The snow provides warmth and cover for mice and voles, who tunnel through the snow and eat the grasses beneath it. Sometimes they have unwanted company—a shrew or weasel in hot pursuit.

In dead of winter, temperatures can drop to 50° below zero and daylight dwindles to about five hours of twilight. On a frigid day, there is no sound except the whisper of the wind and the crunch of snow underfoot. The only disturbance to the snow are tracks made by a prowling fox or wolf, a scurrying mouse, a strolling ptarmigan. The screech of a raven might pierce the crisp day. At night, the dark sky sparkles with northern lights dancing overhead.

Snowmachines are not allowed in the park, so winter visitors travel by ski, snowshoe, or the way people have traveled through this area for

There's more to Denali than June, July, and August. Indeed, winter is Denali's main season, top left. Snow falls, cold descends, some animals migrate south, and others hibernate. A year-round resident, the willow ptarmigan, above, has feathered feet to protect against winter cold. A bull moose, opposite, forages during an early snowstorm near Teklanika. Long legs help moose travel through deep snow.

hundreds of years—by dog team. Native people used dogs to travel to the Denali area to hunt and prospectors used dog teams to haul gear for mining. Harry Karstens and Charles Sheldon used dogs for transportation during their 1907–1908 winter at Toklat. Mountaineers challenging Mount McKinley hired dog teams to haul freight to the mountain's base. Naturally, dogs continue to play an important role during winter months at Denali National Park. Sled dogs from the National Park Service kennel regularly patrol the park and its boundaries. Local dog mushers, too, often journey into Denali, particularly in March when days are long and temperatures rise. Wildlife also begins to react to warmer temperatures. Bears have been spotted out of their dens as early as late March.

Daylight lengthens, temperatures rise, and the land begins to change, but this is only a seasonal variation. Denali National Park and its inhabitants evolve in a physical way, every day. Like a moody child, Denali changes its personality abruptly. Grumbling dark clouds can put a foreboding chill on a sunny, snoozy day. A few hours later, Denali can shake off the bad mood and relax again, enticing with a warm glow as the sun emerges once more.

Glacial rivers continually cut new channels through the gravel of riverbeds. Heavy rains cause mudslides, and rocks regularly tumble down Polychrome Pass. Whole mountainsides change

RON SANFORD

character as flowers bloom for a few weeks, then wither. The ground itself melts under almost twenty-four hours of summer sun, sliding downhill to be locked in place at the next freeze.

Bears dig up patches of tundra looking for roots or ground squirrels. Pikas stash little piles of grass and flowers in tiny rock crevices. Seeds scatter and plants dig in for the next growing season a whole year away. In a matter of weeks, Denali changes costume, from brown, to green, to white. What doesn't change is the natural order of things. The wildness stays the same.

Denali National Park is a pristine place. We must ensure it always stays that way.

There's something magical about seeing a caribou silhouetted against a Denali sky. Opposite, a tundra pool reflects a colorful summer sunrise. These are special moments to be cherished and remembered.

CRAIG BRANDT

Grizzly Bear
Ursus arctos
BOAR, SOW, CUB, PACK OR SLOTH

HABITAT
Home ranges vary at Denali National Park

FOOD
Omnivore: 80% roots, grasses, berries; 20% ground squirrel, moose and caribou calves, rodents, carrion

SIZE/WEIGHT/LIFESPAN
Male: 300–500 pounds; maximum 650 pounds
Female: 200–400 pounds
Maximum height:
6–7 feet standing;
3½ to 4 feet at shoulders
Grizzly bears live to be in their 20s; some have been known to reach age 30

LIFE CYCLES
Mate May–July, at 4–6 years
Gestation period: 6 months
Cubs born January–February in sow's den; cubs weigh less than 2 pounds. Twins common.
Bears enter dens in October; emerge in April–May

MICHAEL GIANNECHINI

Caribou
Rangifer tarandus
BULL, COW, CALF, HERD

HABITAT
Constantly moving, caribou generally (but not always) roam the tundra above timberline

FOOD
Herbivore: willow, dwarf birch, grasses in summer; lichens, moss, dried sedges in winter

SIZE/WEIGHT/LIFESPAN
Male: 350–400 pounds
Female: 175–225 pounds
Maximum height:
3½ to 4 feet at shoulders
Caribou live 11–12 years

LIFE CYCLES
Mate in October, at 3 years
Gestation period: 8 months
One calf born May–June;
Calves weigh 10–15 pounds

HENRY HOLDSWORTH

Dall Sheep
Ovis dalli dalli
RAM, EWE, LAMB, BAND

HABITAT
Alpine ridges, meadows, and steep, rugged slopes

FOOD
Herbivore: flowers, grasses, willows in summer; mosses, lichens in winter

SIZE/WEIGHT/LIFESPAN
125–200 pounds
3 to 3½ feet at shoulder
Dall sheep live 11–14 years

LIFE CYCLES
Mate November to December, at age 3 years
Gestation period: 6 months
One lamb born May–June;
twins are rare

ROBIN BRANDT

Moose
Alces alces gigas
BULL, COW, CALF

HABITAT
River bottoms, willow patches, woodlands

FOOD
Herbivore: Moose eat grasses in spring; willow, aspen, birch in summer; twigs, bark, saplings in winter

SIZE/WEIGHT/LIFESPAN
Male: 1,000–1,500 pounds
Female: 800–1,200 pounds
Maximum height:
7½ feet at shoulders
Moose live 17–20 years

LIFE CYCLES
Mate September–October, from age 2 to 3 years
Gestation period: 8 months
1 to 3 calves born May–June;
Calves weight 28–35 pounds

Gray Wolf
Canis lupus
DOG, BITCH, PUP, PACK

HABITAT
Throughout the park, one w may range 25 to 150 square miles; a pack may range 20(to 600 square miles

FOOD
Carnivore: rodents, hare, beaver, birds, moose, caribo sheep, carrion

SIZE/WEIGHT/LIFESPAN
Male: 85–115 pounds
Female: 75–105 pounds
Maximum height:
2½ feet at shoulders
Wolves live 9–12 years

LIFE CYCLES
Mate February–March, at age 2 years
Gestation period: 63 days
2 to 10 pups (average 5) born in May